1. Background

The purpose of this Information Publication is to provide owners, operators, sponsors, and other entities charged with oversight of GA landing facilities with a set of security best practices and a method for determining when and where these enhancements would be appropriate. Regarding GA, a few definitions are in order:

- GA, as used in this document, means all civil aviation except for scheduled passenger and scheduled cargo service and military aviation.
- Airports, as used in this document, means an area of land or water that is used or intended to be used for the landing and takeoff of aircraft, and includes its buildings and facilities, if any. However, this document does not apply to airports required to comply with the provisions of 49 CFR 1542 or military airports.

This document does not contain regulatory language. It is not intended to suggest that any recommendations or guidelines contained herein might be considered as mandatory requirements to be imposed upon GA facilities or operators, nor are these recommendations and guidelines intended to suggest any specific or general criteria to be met in order to qualify for Federal funding. The intent of this document is to provide a tool that enables GA landing facility managers to assess vulnerabilities and tailor appropriate security measures to their environment -- not to 'stigmatize' airports in any way.

Recognizing that every GA landing facility is unique, there are recommendations and guidelines contained in this document that might be considered highly beneficial in one airport environment while being virtually impossible to implement at another facility. The purpose of the document is to provide an extensive list of options, ideas, and suggestions for the airport operator, sponsor, tenant and/or user to choose from when considering security enhancements for GA facilities. When stating in this document that a measure "should" be used it means the measure is recommended to the extent it is consistent with the airport's circumstances as discussed throughout this document. The Transportation Security Administration (TSA) intends that this document be used to provide effective and reasonable security enhancements at GA facilities across the Nation.

To date there have been numerous initiatives undertaken by the GA industry to develop GA airport security guidelines such as awareness programs, reporting methods, and educational courses. These efforts have been considered by TSA and are reflected in this guidance document.

Please note that throughout this document many airport terms are used that are the same as or similar to those terms used when describing airports required to comply with the security regulations outlined in 49 CFR Part 1542. It is not the intent of this document to recommend that GA landing facilities meet the same security requirements as commercial service airports. However, on occasion it is necessary to use terminology that airport operators are already familiar with in order to facilitate readers' understanding. Additionally, references are made to Federal Aviation Administration (FAA) guidance materials normally related to commercial service airports and operations. These documents are provided as reference material but may not necessarily constitute an appropriate approach to GA security at your facility.

1.1.   The GA Industry

As previously stated, as used in this document, GA encompasses all civil aviation, except military aviation and passenger and scheduled cargo service. Some basic statistics available regarding the industry:

- Reportedly more than 19,000 landing facilities nationwide, including heliports, lakes, and dirt landing strips in remote wilderness areas as well as GA airports near urban settings that rival the size and scope of some air carrier airports.
- Over 200,000 GA aircraft in the U.S. are responsible for 75% of all air traffic.
- These FAA certificated and non-certificated aircraft range from one-person ultralights and powered parachutes with extremely limited range and payload capabilities to helicopters, seaplanes, vintage, fabric-and-wood biplanes, experimental airplanes, four-seat single-engine airplanes, twin turboprops, and large and small business jets.
- The GA industry accounts for over 1.3 million jobs, with nearly $20 billion in annual earnings. Its direct and indirect economic impact exceeds $102 billion annually.
- More than 630,000 certificated pilots are in the U.S. Airmen Registry, most of whom conduct GA flight operations.
- Approximately 145 million passengers annually are transported in GA aircraft of all sizes for business and personal reasons.
- Notionally an estimated 58% of all GA flights are conducted for business and corporate travel.
- Commercial, non-scheduled flights (charters) are also a component of GA, with more than 22,000 pilots flying some 14,700 aircraft for this industry segment during 2001 alone.
- GA aircraft are used for a wide range of flight operations including personal/family transportation, training, MEDEVAC, transporting medical supplies, emergency services, rescue operations, wildlife surveys, traffic reporting, agricultural aviation, firefighting, and law enforcement.

(Sources: December 2003 FAA Administrator's Fact Book; GA Serving America www.gaservingamerica.com; National Air Transportation Association)

Because of the wide variety and scope of GA aircraft and landing locations, any approach to implementing security guidelines must consider the various types of flight operations as well as the size of aircraft involved, among other factors. Therefore, a flexible, common-sense approach to GA airport security is important if the industry is to retain its economic vitality.

1.2. The Aviation Security Advisory Committee (ASAC)

Following the 1988 Pan American World Airways Flight 103 tragedy, it was determined a need existed for all segments of the aviation industry to have input into future aviation security considerations. In response, the Aviation Security Advisory Committee (ASAC) was established in 1989 and was managed by the Federal Aviation Administration (FAA). After the terrorist attacks of September 11, 2001, Congress enacted the Aviation and Transportation Security Act (ATSA), which created the TSA. Congress established TSA to develop, regulate, and enforce transportation security standards for all modes of transportation. Consistent with this mission, Congress transferred the bulk of FAA's civil aviation security responsibilities to TSA. Accordingly, sponsorship of the ASAC was also transferred to TSA.

In April 2003, TSA requested ASAC to establish a working group made up of industry stakeholders to develop guidelines for security enhancements at the nation's private and public use GA landing facilities. TSA made this request because, in the absence of a unified set of federal security standards for GA airports, some state and local governments had begun developing their own airport-related security requirements. TSA recognized that this could result in varied state and local security requirements that could pose an unnecessary burden on airport owners and operators while leaving security gaps in other locations. TSA believed that a better approach would be to address GA airports (both public and private use) in a collaborative forum in order to develop a set of industry endorsed guidelines and "best practices" that are tailored to broad categories of airports.

The Working Group represented the GA industry as a whole. Participating members included:

• Aircraft Owners & Pilots Association (AOPA)
• Airport Consultants Council (ACC)
• American Association of Airport Executives (AAAE)
• Experimental Aircraft Association (EAA)
• GA Manufacturers Association (GAMA)
• Helicopter Association International (HAI)
• National Air Transportation Association (NATA)
• National Association of State Aviation Officials (NASAO)
• National Business Aviation Association (NBAA)
• United States Parachute Association (USPA)

Additionally, GA airport managers and representatives of various state government aviation agencies fully participated in the working group's activities.

1.3.   GA Airport Vulnerability

Historically, GA airports have not been subject to federal rules regarding airport security. Prior to September 11, 2001, the federal government's role in airport security focused exclusively on those airports serving scheduled operations. Now, however, TSA must examine all aspects of the transportation system for vulnerabilities to terrorist activities. To date TSA has not required GA airports to implement security measures except for those facilities located within the Washington DC Airspace Defense Identification Zone Flight Restricted Zone. Nevertheless, many GA airport managers commonly implement basic security measures found throughout the nation's airports. Examples include fencing and access control devices for vehicle and pedestrian gates, daily airfield inspections, landside and airfield signage, and public awareness programs for educating the aviation community as well as the general public on the safe and secure use of the facility.

TSA has not taken a position that GA airports and aircraft are a threat, in and of themselves. However, as vulnerabilities within other areas of aviation have been reduced, GA may be perceived as a more attractive target and consequently more vulnerable to misuse by terrorists. TSA believes that the security guidelines outlined in this document will help airport managers and aircraft operators determine which security measures they should take at their particular facility to reduce vulnerabilities and encourage the adoption of consistent and appropriate security measures across the nation. TSA also believes that these security guidelines must be federally endorsed to discourage a hodgepodge of state and local guidelines.

By definition the term GA includes a broad range of aircraft and aviation activity. Not surprisingly, GA airports vary greatly in size, function and operational characteristics. Just as all commercial service airports differ in their security needs the same is true with GA airports. TSA understands that one size security will not fit the entire spectrum of GA airports. For example, a privately owned landing strip in a rural area would not need to implement the same security measures as a large corporate GA airport near a major metropolitan area. While the potential for misuse of an aircraft operating from the rural airport exists, required adherence to a single requirement across the nation is physically and economically impossible and clearly not reasonable. TSA must instead focus on managing the risk associated with GA facilities recognizing the characteristics that define each facility.

The ability (physically and financially) of GA airports to voluntarily implement security improvements varies greatly. The majority of these facilities are not self-sustaining in the same manner as commercial service airports. Consequently, the decision to implement security measures must include consideration of economic feasibility and reasonableness.

2. Airport Characteristics

Airport Characteristics Measurement Tool

In order to assess which security enhancements are most appropriate for a GA landing facility, consideration must be given to those elements that make the airport unique. The most appropriate party to do this would be the person or persons with day-to-day operational control over the facility. This could be a state official, airport manager, or fixed base operator (FBO). In any case, the party doing the assessment should be intimately familiar with the airport, its activities, and the surrounding areas.

To assist in this effort, TSA has developed an Airport Characteristics Measurement Tool (found in Appendix A) that can be used to determine where in the risk spectrum the facility lies. The tool is a list of airport characteristics that potentially affect a facility's security posture. Each of the characteristics is assigned a point ranking, the idea being that certain characteristics affect the security at an airport more so than others.

The characteristics have been broken down into the following categories:

- Airport Location – A facility's proximity to mass population areas or sensitive sites can affect its security posture. **For the purpose of this guidance we are considering a mass population area to be an area with a total metropolitan population of at least 100,000 people. A sensitive site is defined as an area which would be considered a key asset or critical infrastructure of the United States. Sensitive sites can include certain military installations, nuclear and chemical plants, centers of government, monuments and iconic structures, and/or international ports.** Distance from such sites directly affects the ability of responding agencies to effectively react to an event. The further away from a potential target, the greater the response time available to responding agencies.

- Based Aircraft – A smaller number of based aircraft increases the likelihood that illegal activities would be identified more quickly than at airports with a large number of based aircraft. In addition, airports with based aircraft of over 12,500 pounds warrant greater scrutiny.

- Runways – Airports with longer paved runways are able to serve larger aircraft and consequently should be more security conscious. Conversely, because shorter, unpaved runways are not practical for use by large aircraft in many weather conditions, they may present a less attractive launching point for terrorist activities. **Airport operators at facilities with multiple runways should only consider the longest operational runway on the airport.**

  Please note: TSA recognizes that airports at higher elevations may need longer runways to accommodate even the smallest of aircraft. It is not the intent of this document to assess points for a longer runway if it is unrealistic that the runway could be used for larger aircraft operations. Individuals using the Airport Characteristics Measurement Tool should understand that the baseline of the Tool was developed to consider aircraft performance at approximately sea level.

- Operations – The number and types of operations that are conducted at an airport call for different approaches to security. **Consider all operations including those operations that are only infrequently conducted at your airport.**

Additionally, there is a distinct difference between "public use" airports and "private use" airports. Privately-owned, private-use GA airports receive no public funds and most state government aviation agencies currently have no authority to regulate them. However, TSA believes that some of the guidelines in this report would be beneficial to enhancing the security at these facilities as well.

To use the tool, you should choose those characteristics that apply to your facility. Each of the characteristics is assigned a point value from 0-5 as shown in the Appendix A Tool. Assess points for **every** characteristic that applies to your facility (except for runway length considerations, there may be more than one selection in each category) and total the number of points scored.

Example 1

Security Characteristics	Public Use Airport/Heliport
Small, rural, public use field located a significant distance from any sensitive sites	0
15 based aircraft	1
2500' runway	4
Asphalt runway	1
Flight training is conducted on airfield	3
Total	9

Example 2

Security Characteristics	Public Use Airport/Heliport
Airport within 30nm of a sensitive site	4
Within the boundaries of Class B airspace	3
50 based aircraft	2
5000' runway	5
Asphalt runway	1
More than 50,000 aircraft operations per year	4
Part 135 operations	3
Flight training is conducted on airfield	3
Rental aircraft	4
Total	29

Suggested Airport Security Enhancements

Appendix B contains groupings of security enhancements that may be appropriate for those facilities scoring within a certain point range on the Airport Characteristics Measurement Tool. The lists of suggested security enhancements are grouped according to the point range totals derived using the Measurement Tool. These lists are by no means complete for every facility, nor are they the only method for improving security. They are suggestions that could be useful at these locations. They should not be used as the sole means of determining what security precautions are appropriate. Instead, airport owners and operators should rely on their experience and intimate knowledge of their facility, applying those items that are both reasonable and effective.

This list is an assessment of the most significant characteristics relating to GA airport security. The scope and breadth of GA landing facilities precludes any one document from capturing all characteristics relevant to all GA airports. Users are advised to consider all characteristics germane to security at their particular facility when using the Airport Characteristics Measurement Tool.

Mitigating Characteristics

TSA also recognizes that some characteristics of GA airports actually serve the purpose of enhancing security, such as having a police presence on the airport property. Other characteristics may negate the need for certain security measures, such as if all of an airport's runways are grass. Airport operators should use their best judgment when considering mitigating characteristics and their effect on which security enhancements are to be implemented at their airport. Some examples of mitigating circumstances are:

- Operating air traffic control tower on the field
- 24/7 airport staffing
- Federal, state, local, or contract law enforcement on airport property
- All based aircraft under 1500 lbs

- All runways are grass
- Restricted access to the airport
- Require ID badges
- Documented security Procedures

3. Recommendations

Managers and operators of GA airports are encouraged to use the recommended guidelines in this report to enhance the security of their respective facilities. Intrinsic in these recommended guidelines is the concept that GA airports are extremely diverse and that appropriate security measures can be determined only after careful examination of an individual airport. The key findings of the report are encompassed in the following areas:

- Personnel
- Aircraft
- Airports and Facilities
- Surveillance
- Security Procedures and Communications
- Specialty Operations

3.1.   Personnel

3.1.1. Passengers/Visitors

A key point to remember regarding GA passengers is that the persons on board these flights are generally better known to airport personnel and aircraft operators than the typical passenger on a commercial airliner. Recreational GA passengers are typically friends, family, or acquaintances of the pilot in command. Charter/sightseeing passengers typically will meet with the pilot or other flight department personnel well in advance of any flights. Suspicious activities such as use of cash for flights or probing or inappropriate questions are more likely to be quickly noted and authorities could be alerted. For corporate operations, typically all parties onboard the aircraft are known to the pilots. Airport operators should develop methods by which individuals visiting the airport can be escorted into and out of aircraft movement and parking areas. By utilizing common sense suggestions, the GA community can help ensure the security of their airport. Prior to boarding, the pilot in command should ensure that:

- The identity of all occupants is verified,
- All occupants are aboard at the invitation of the owner/operator, and
- All baggage and cargo is known to the occupants.

3.1.2. Flight Schools and Student Pilots

We now know that the September 11 terrorists trained at flight schools in Florida, Arizona, and Minnesota. This has raised concerns among the public and federal law enforcement organizations about flight school security and how it can be improved.

In response the federal government and the aviation industry have developed the following recommendations designed to enhance positive control of the aircraft before movement, when an instructor is ready to accompany the student. Flight schools should:

- Require flight students to use proper entrances and exits to ramp areas. If access controls are available, consider having flight school personnel allow access to ramp areas only after establishing positive identification of flight students.
- Establish positive identification of student pilots prior to every flight lesson.
- Control aircraft ignition keys so that the student cannot start the aircraft until the instructor is ready for the flight to begin.
- Limit student pilot access to aircraft keys until the student pilot has reached an appropriate point in the training curriculum.
- Consider having any student pilot check in with a specific employee (i.e. dispatcher, aircraft scheduler, flight instructor, or other "management" official) before being allowed access to parked aircraft.
- Have the student sign or initial a form and not receive keys until an instructor or other "management official" also signs or initials.
- When available, use a different ignition key from the door lock key. The instructor would provide the ignition key when he or she arrives at the aircraft.

TSA is developing a security awareness training program for use by flight schools that may also be used by GA airports. The training program will provide information on suspicious behavior patterns, appropriate responses to such behavior, and GA airport watch programs. The training program will be available electronically on the TSA GA website (www.tsa.gov/public/display?theme=180) in the summer of 2004. The GA website also will contain information regarding any general threats to GA airports or aircraft and major incidents involving GA airports or aircraft.

3.1.3. Aircraft Renters

A very large proportion of GA aircraft are used for rental purposes. At most airports, regular aircraft renters are fairly well known, and new renters are typically required by insurance agencies to complete a flight check which ascertains their ability to safely operate rental aircraft. Both of these factors may serve as a deterrent to using GA aircraft for terrorist purposes. However, developing and documenting standard procedures and ensuring flight school employees are educated in the procedures further enhances flight school security.

- The identity of an individual renting an aircraft should be verified by checking an individual's government-issued photo ID as well as his or her airman certificate and current medical certificate necessary for that operation.
- In addition to any aircraft-specific operational and training requirements, a first-time rental customer should be familiarized with local airport operations, including security procedures used at the facility.
- Operators providing rental aircraft should be vigilant for suspicious activities and report them to appropriate officials.

3.1.4. Transient Pilots

Airport personnel should strive to establish procedures to identify non-based pilots and aircraft using their facilities. One helpful method would be for airport or FBO operators to establish sign-in/sign-out procedures for all transient operators and associate them with their parked aircraft. Having assigned spots for transient parking areas can help to easily identify transient aircraft on an apron.

3.2.   *Aircraft*

The main goal of enhancing GA airport security is to prevent the intentional misuse of GA aircraft for terrorist purposes. Proper securing of aircraft is the most basic method of enhancing GA airport security. Pilots should employ multiple methods of securing their aircraft to make it as difficult as possible for an unauthorized person to gain access to it.

Some basic methods of securing a GA aircraft include:

- Ensuring that door locks are consistently used to prevent unauthorized access or tampering with the aircraft.
- Using keyed ignitions where appropriate.
- Storing the aircraft in a hangar, if available, and locking hangar doors.
- Using an auxiliary lock to further protect aircraft from unauthorized use. Commercially available options for auxiliary locks include locks for propellers, throttle, and tie-downs.
- Ensuring that aircraft ignition keys are not stored inside the aircraft.

3.3.   Airports/Facilities

3.3.1. Hangars

Storage in hangars is one of the most effective methods of securing GA aircraft. TSA recognizes that hangar space at many airports is limited. However, every attempt should be made to utilize hangars when available and ensure that all hangar/personnel doors are secured when unattended.

Hangars should be properly marked and numbered for ease of emergency response. These areas are also a good place to install security and informational signs. Hangar locks that have keys that are easily obtained or duplicated should be avoided. Hangar locks should be rekeyed with every new tenant. Proper lighting around hangar areas should be installed. As an additional security measure alarm and intrusion detection systems could also aid in the security of hangars.

3.3.2. Locks

Regardless of its quality or cost a lock is simply a delaying device and not a complete bar to entry. As important as the choice of lock is, the decision where to install locks is more important. Such factors to consider may include:

- Is the object to be locked indoors or outdoors?
- How many people will need to use the lock (i.e. would a combination be better than issuing keys)?
- Would a certain type of lock impede access in high traffic areas?
- How secure should the area be made?
- Is the area monitored?
- How often will codes, keys, or locks need to be changed for persons needing access (e.g. new hangar tenants, those with tiedown agreements needing ramp access, etc.)?
- Will use of a lock interfere with fire code egress requirements?

A more detailed discussion of locks and their use can be found in Appendix C.

3.3.3. Perimeter Control

To delineate and adequately protect security areas from unauthorized access it is important to consider boundary measures such as fencing, walls, or other physical barriers, electronic boundaries (e.g. sensor lines, alarms), and/or natural barriers. Physical barriers can be used to deter and delay the access of unauthorized persons onto sensitive areas of airports. Such structures are usually permanent and are designed to be a visual and psychological deterrent as well as a physical barrier. They also serve to meet safety requirements in many cases. Where possible, security fencing or other physical barriers should be aligned with security area boundaries.

The choice of an appropriate security boundary design is not only affected by the cost of equipment, installation, and maintenance, but also by effectiveness and functionality, that is, its ability to prevent unauthorized access.

However, it is important to note that perimeter control methods alone will not necessarily prevent a determined intruder from entering, nor may they be appropriate for every facility. The strength of any security mechanism is dependent on the airport's overall security plan. Expending resources on an unnecessary security enhancement (e.g. complete perimeter fencing, and access controls) instead of a more facility specific, reasonable, and more effective method (e.g. tiedown chains with locks) may actually be detrimental to an airport's overall security posture.

More specific information on perimeter control can be found in Appendices D and E.

3.3.4. Lighting

Protective lighting provides a means of continuing a degree of protection from theft, vandalism, or other illegal activity at night. Security lighting systems should be connected to an emergency power source, if available. Requirements for protective lighting of airports depend upon the local situation and the areas to be protected. A careful analysis of security lighting requirements should be based on the need for good visibility and the following criteria: employee recognition and badge identification, vehicle access, detection of intruders, and deterrent to illegal entry. Protective lighting is generally inexpensive to maintain, and when properly employed, may provide airport personnel with added protection from surprise by a determined intruder. However, when developing any security lighting plan care should be taken to ensure that lighting does not interfere with aircraft operations.

Consider installing outdoor area lighting to help improve the security of aircraft parking and hangar areas, fuel storage areas, airport access points; and other appropriate areas.

A more detailed discussion of lighting can be found in Appendix F.

3.3.5. Signs

The use of signs provides a deterrent by warning of facility boundaries as well notifying of the consequences for violation. Signs along a fence line should be located such that when standing at one sign, the observer is able to see the next sign in both directions. While signs for security purposes should be designed to draw attention, it also should be coordinated with other airport signs for style and consistency when possible. Signs should be constructed of durable materials, contrasting colors, and reflective material where appropriate. Use as concise language as possible.

Wording may include – but is not limited to – warnings against trespassing, unauthorized use of aircraft and tampering with aircraft, and reporting of suspicious activity. Signage should include phone numbers of the nearest responding law enforcement agency, 9-1-1, or TSA's 1-866-GA-SECUR (see section 3.4.2), whichever is appropriate.

Many locations with access control or Closed Circuit Television (CCTV) equipment may warrant signage for directional, legal, or law enforcement purposes (e.g. "Alarm will sound if opened", "Authorized personnel only", "Notice: All activities in this area are being monitored and recorded", etc.).

For more information refer to Advisory Circular (AC) No: 150/5360-12D, Airport Signing and Graphics. At international airports, designers and airport authorities may also wish to consult the International Civil Aviation Organization (ICAO) Document 9430-C/1080, International Signs to Provide Guidelines to Persons at Airports.

3.3.6. Identification System

Some airport operators may wish to consider implementing a method of identifying airport employees or authorized tenant access to various areas of the airport. Currently, there are many systems on the market that may accomplish this. They can range from a simple laminated identification card that includes a photograph of an individual to a sophisticated swipe card with various biometric data. With any identification system, procedures should be developed that include ensuring control and accountability of the media.

Some elements that could be part of an identification system include:

- A full-face image
- The individual's full name
- Airport name
- Employer
- A unique identification number
- The scope of the individual access and movement privileges (e.g. color coding)
- A clear expiration date

A vehicle identification system may be developed. Such a system can assist airport personnel and law enforcement in identifying authorized vehicles. Vehicles can be identified through use of decals, stickers, or hang tags. Decals should be nontransferable; that is, they should not be capable of being removed without destroying their integrity. These systems should also be used to indicate access authorization where appropriate, such as by numbering or color-coding. Issuing authorities should also attempt to make current stickers/decals easily distinguished from expired ones. In addition, any decal application form should contain owner contact information that may be used in the event of an emergency.

More suggestions for establishing an identification system can be found in AC-107-1, "Aviation Security – Airports".

3.3.7. Airport Planning

Planning for security should be an integral part of any project undertaken at an airport. The most efficient and cost effective method of instituting security measures into any facility or operation is thorough advance planning and continuous monitoring throughout the project. Selecting, constructing, or modifying a facility without considering the security implications can result in costly modifications and delays. Airport operators should consider addressing future security needs such as access controls and lighting enhancements when planning new hangars or terminal buildings. Security concerns should be included and addressed in airport facility and land leases, airport rules and regulations, and the Minimum Standards document. In addition, airport construction projects can affect airfield security. Construction personnel and vehicle access during projects should be considered.

3.4.   Surveillance

3.4.1. Airport Community Watch Program

The vigilance of airport users is one of the most prevalent methods of enhancing security at GA airports. Typically, the user population is familiar with those individuals who have a valid purpose for being on the airport property. Consequently, new faces are quickly noticed. Teaching an airport's users and tenants what to look for with regard to unauthorized and potentially illegal activities is essential to effectively utilizing this resource. Airport managers can either utilize an existing airport watch program or establish their own airport specific plan. A watch program should include elements similar to those listed below. These recommendations are not all-inclusive. Additional measures that are specific to each airport should be added as appropriate, including:

- Coordinate the program with all appropriate stakeholders including airport officials, pilots, businesses and/or other airport users.
- Hold periodic meetings with the airport community.
- Develop and circulate reporting procedures to all who have a regular presence on the airport.

- Encourage proactive participation in aircraft and facility security and heightened awareness measures. This should include encouraging airport and line staff to 'query' unknowns on ramps, near aircraft, etc.
- Post signs promoting the program, warning that the airport is watched. Include appropriate emergency phone numbers on the sign.
- Install a bulletin board for posting security information and meeting notices.
- Provide training to all involved for recognizing suspicious activity and appropriate response tactics. This could include the use of a video or other media for training. The following are some recommended training topics:
  - Aircraft with unusual or unauthorized modifications.
  - Persons loitering for extended periods in the vicinity of parked aircraft, in pilot lounges, or other areas deemed inappropriate.
  - Pilots who appear to be under the control of another person.
  - Persons wishing to rent aircraft without presenting proper credentials or identification.
  - Persons who present apparently valid credentials but who do not display a corresponding level of aviation knowledge.
  - Any pilot who makes threats or statements inconsistent with normal uses of aircraft.
  - Events or circumstances that do not fit the pattern of lawful, normal activity at an airport.
- Utilize local law enforcement for airport security community education.
- Encourage tenants to make their staff aware of the airport watch programs.

3.4.2. Reporting Procedures

It is essential that every airport employee, tenant, and user is familiar with reporting unusual or suspicious circumstances on airport property. There are three basic ways that persons can report suspect activities. First is to airport management. Oftentimes questions regarding the legitimacy of an activity can be quickly and easily resolved by bringing it to the attention of an airport employee.

A second method is to utilize the GA-SECURE Hotline. TSA developed and implemented a GA hotline in partnership with the National Response Center. 866-GA-SECUR (1-866-427-3287) was launched on December 2, 2002 and operates 24 hours per day 7 days per week. The GA Hotline serves as a centralized reporting system for general aviation pilots, airport operators, and maintenance technicians wishing to report suspicious activity at their airfield.

The third and most obvious method is to contact local law enforcement using a local phone number or by dialing 911. In instances where the situation could potentially turn dangerous all pilots are strongly encouraged to use this method. However, after contacting 911 or airport management TSA also requests that callers contact the GA Hotline in order to ensure that information surrounding the incident reaches the National Response Center.

3.4.3. Airport Security Committee

Airport management should consider establishing an Airport Security Committee. This Committee should be composed of airport tenants and users drawn from all segments of the airport community. The main goal of this group is to involve airport stakeholders in developing effective and reasonable security measures and disseminating timely security information. Meetings should be held regularly for the purpose of giving coordinated direction to the overall airport security program.

3.4.4. Law Enforcement Officer (LEO) Support

It is imperative that airport operators establish and maintain a liaison with appropriate law enforcement agencies including local, state, and federal. These organizations can better serve the airport operator when they are familiar with airport operating procedures, facilities, and normal activities. Procedures may be developed to have local LEOs regularly or randomly patrol ramps and aircraft hangar areas, with increased patrols during periods of heightened security.

Airport operators should communicate and educate local law enforcement agencies on operational and security procedures at the airport. This may include:

- Recognizing proper airport credentials (e.g. airport ID badges, airmen certificates).
- Recognizing those airport users authorized to drive on the ramp.
- Notifying LEOs as to how they can obtain airport access (e.g. who has gate keys, access codes).
- Educating LEOs on airport speed limits, aircraft right-of-way procedures, and other "normal" operations.
- Issuing airport maps with a detailed facility index.
- Recognizing "normal" airport operations.

3.4.5. Closed Circuit Television (CCTV)

Although CCTV is used for many purposes, its most common use is for surveillance. CCTV systems make it possible for fewer individuals to maintain a constant watch on all areas of the facility. These systems may even provide an alternative to fencing as a method of perimeter security. In conjunction with a perimeter fence, CCTV may also deter security breaches at airports, and may provide an improved response when breaches do occur. Additionally, CCTV video recorders may provide a visual record that can be used to document activities that become the subject of investigations. However, the inherent weakness of this system is that it must be monitored to be effective. CCTV may be appropriate only at busier, more complex airports.

3.4.6. Intrusion Detection Systems (IDS)

IDS are becoming more and more popular as a method for providing GA airport security. The inherent benefit to such systems is that they can replace the need for physical security personnel to patrol an entire facility or perimeter. Typically, such systems are constantly monitored by a contracting company. If an intrusion or some other specified event (e.g. fire or power outage) is detected, the system administrator notifies police, fire, and/or airport management. Costs vary depending upon the type of system, monitoring fees, and equipment. Such systems can be used to secure terminals, hangars, or other airport facilities, or be used to monitor perimeter security and access points.

3.5.   Security Procedures & Communications

3.5.1. Security Procedures

GA airport managers/operators may find it helpful to develop written security procedures. Many of these security initiatives are already being conducted on airfields but have not been formalized into a documented program. Documentation provides managers with a traceable and auditable method of ensuring airport employees and tenants are aware of and understand security issues. Such a protocol should minimally consist of, but not be limited to, airport and local law enforcement contact information, including alternates when available, and utilization of a program to increase airport user awareness of security precautions such as Airport Watch.

Because security procedures may contain sensitive information, the airport operator should limit access to them to the extent possible.

A procedures template can be found in Appendix G.

3.5.2. Threat Level Increases

The Homeland Security Advisory System (HSAS) is a mechanism for the Department of Homeland Security to disseminate information regarding the risk of terrorist acts throughout the nation. It provides airport operators with information to implement increased security measures during times of heightened alert and to reduce security procedures at lower threat levels.

A written GA security procedure can include reference to and be coordinated with appropriate local response plans as prepared for the specific region in which the landing facility is located. The protocol should emphasize such critical elements as awareness, prevention, preparation, response, and recovery. Intrinsic in these recommended guidelines is the concept that each GA airport is unique. Airport operators are encouraged to develop response procedures appropriate to their facility. During times of lower alert levels airport operators may wish to do the following:

- Develop preparedness plans, emergency contact lists, and training programs to ensure key elements of HSAS and preparedness plans are presented to all employees.
- Review and update any previously developed preparedness plans, emergency contact lists, and training programs.
- Communicate with appropriate local federal agency representatives (e.g. DHS, FBI, and TSA).
- Conduct surveillance of facility property, buildings, and aircraft.
- Coordinate emergency plans as appropriate with nearby jurisdictions.
- Hold security committee meetings to ensure timely dissemination of security/threat information.

Under most circumstances, the measures for increased alert levels (Orange or Red) are not intended to be sustained for substantial periods. Appropriate actions may include:

- Conducting all measures taken at lower threat condition.
- Limiting facility access points.
- Making regular surveillance patrols of facility property, buildings, and aircraft.
- Increasing surveillance of critical locations.
- Coordinating necessary security efforts with federal, state, and local law enforcement agencies or any National Guard or other appropriate organizations.
- Preparing to execute contingency procedures, as appropriate.
- Ensuring positive identification of pilots and tenants.
- Assigning emergency response personnel, pre-positioning, and mobilize specially trained teams or resources.
- Closing the facility.

3.5.3. Threat Communication System

The development of a comprehensive contact list is recommended to be included in any airport security procedures. The list should be distributed all appropriate individuals. The following phone numbers should be included on the contact list (include after hour contact numbers where appropriate):

- Landing facility operator
- Landing facility manager
- Individual with responsibility for facility security

- Local Police or County Sheriff Department (List all responding LEO Agencies)
- State Aviation Director
- County/City Emergency Manager
- State Police
- Fire Department
- State Office of Public Safety/Homeland Security
- FBI
- Local FAA contact
- Local TSA contact (that is, Federal Security Director or designee)
- Any other appropriate organization

Additionally, in the event of a security incident, it is essential that first responders and airport management have the capability to communicate. Where possible, coordinate radio communication and establish common frequencies and procedures to establish a radio communications network with local law enforcement.

Also important to the communication process is a means by which all new security policies, procedures, and alerts are communicated to tenants and other airport users. One method of accomplishing this is to conduct regular meetings with airport tenants and the flying public to discuss security issues and challenges, establishing a centralized area for posting of security information, or even developing an email alert system.

3.6.   *Specialty Operations*

3.6.1. Agricultural Aircraft Operations

TSA recognizes the proactive steps taken by agricultural aircraft operators to secure the industry. TSA suggests that each owner/operator take appropriate steps to secure agricultural aircraft when unattended, including:

- Use multiple devices to secure agricultural aircraft such as throttle and control locks, propeller locks, and hidden ignition switches.
- Store aircraft in hangars with electronic security systems and steel doors.
- Park heavy equipment in the front and back of agricultural aircraft when hangers are not available for storage.

Additional security measures can be found on the National Agricultural Aircraft Association's website at: http://www.agaviation.org/

3.6.2. Airport Tenant Facilities

For those airports with a perimeter fence, many airport tenant facilities have access to the aircraft parking and movement and public areas of the airport through their building. Typically, the tenant leasing the facility is responsible for security. However their access controls may also be incorporated into the airport's security procedures and/or alarm and reporting system. Airport operators should coordinate with their tenants to ensure that any security procedures or systems do not conflict or leave gaps. For example, airport management should coordinate and ensure security procedures exist and are harmonized with maintenance facilities that have access on both the public side of the fence and the aircraft parking and movement areas.

3.6.3. Aircraft and Vehicle Fueling Facilities

Fuel farms are normally placed in as remote a location of the airport as possible for safety and convenience purposes. If feasible, use security fencing, lighting, and access controls whenever possible to control movement in these areas. Trucks used to transfer fuel to aircraft should be secured when not in use. This includes controlling fuel truck keys and not leaving keys in trucks while unattended. Consider marshalling fuel trucks in an easily monitored location.

3.6.4. Military Facilities

Some airports may have adjacent or on-airport military facilities such as military Reserve, National Guard, or active duty units. Since each of these situations is unique, and since these facilities are often at least partly within the aircraft movement area, detailed coordination between the airport and the military facility must occur for security procedures and responses. Typical areas of coordination include access control, badging and background check requirements, areas of access, security patrol boundaries, security response responsibilities, and joint and/or shared security system data and equipment.

Appendix A – Airport Characteristics Measurement Tool

Security Characteristics	Assessment Scale	
	Public Use Airports/Heliports	Private Use Airports/Heliports
Location		
Within 30 nm of mass population areas[1]	5	3
Within 30 nm of a sensitive site[2]	4	2
Falls within outer perimeter of Class B airspace	3	1
Falls within the boundaries of restricted airspace	3	1
Based Aircraft		
Greater than 101 based aircraft	3	1
26-100 based aircraft	2	-
11-25 based aircraft	1	-
10 or fewer based aircraft	-	-
Based aircraft over 12,500 lbs	3	1
Runways[3, 4]		
Runway length equal to or greater than 5000 feet	5	3
Runway length less than 5000 feet, Greater than 2001 Feet	4	2
Runway length 2000 feet or less	2	-
Asphalt or concrete runway	1	-
Operations		
Over 50,000 annual aircraft operations	4	2
Part 135 operations	3	1
Part 137 operations	3	1
Part 125 operations	3	1
Flight training	3	1
Flight training in aircraft over 12,500 lbs	4	2
Rental aircraft	4	2
Maintenance, Repair, and Overhaul facilities conducting long term storage of aircraft over 12,500 lbs	4	2
Total		

Assess points for every characteristic that applies to your facility.

1. Mass population area - Area with a total metropolitan population of at least 100,000 people.
2. Sensitive sites - Areas which would be considered key assets or critical infrastructure of the United States. Sensitive sites can include certain military installations, nuclear and chemical plants, centers of government, monuments and iconic structures, and/or international ports.
3. Facilities with multiple runways should only consider the longest runway on the airport.
4. Airports at higher elevations may need longer runways to accommodate even the smallest of aircraft. It is not the intent of this document to assess points for a longer runway if it is unrealistic that the runway could be used for larger aircraft operations.

Appendix B – Suggested Airport Security Enhancements

Points/Suggested Guidelines			
>45	25-44	15-24	0-14
• Fencing (Section 3.3.3) • Hangars (Section 3.3.1) • CCTV (Section 3.4.5) • Intrusion Detection System (Section 3.4.6)			
• Access Controls (Section 3.3.3) • Lighting System (Section 3.3.4) • Personnel ID system (Section 3.3.6) • Vehicle ID system (Section 3.3.6) • Challenge Procedures (Section 3.4.1)			
• LEO Support (Section 3.4.4) • Security Committee (Section 3.4.3) • Transient Pilot Sign-In/Out Procedures (Section 3.1.4)			
• Signs (Section 3.3.5) • Documented Security Procedures (Section 3.5.1) • Positive Passenger/Cargo/Baggage ID (Section 3.1.1) • All Aircraft Secured (Section 3.2) • Community Watch Program (Section 3.4.1) • Contact List (Section 3.5.3)			

Appendix C – Locks

Many ingenious methods have been developed to open locks surreptitiously. Some locks require considerable time and expert manipulation for covert opening but all will succumb to force and the proper tools. Further, many locks can be bypassed either because of poor construction of the lock, poor building construction, or improper installation.

Locks are an integral part of barriers and their security. In addition to their physiological deterrence, their physical strength and resistance to all but the most determined thief provides security in itself. In addition, the loss in time and usual added noise will give increased probability of detection.

It is important that the manager of a facility know each employee who has access to each lock. Key control is as important as the use of locks. There are various types of locks that may be employed at an airport:

- Combination Locks - Combination padlocks can be designed with either fixed or changeable combination mechanisms. However, care should be taken when employing these locks in an area exposed to the elements. Lock combinations should be changed regularly.
- Cipher Locks - A variety of cipher (push button) locks are available. The use of these locks should be limited to controlling access in manned areas as lock codes can be given to unauthorized users. Both electrical and mechanical cipher locks are available. Each may be used with electric release latches, and doors with this type of lock should be equipped with automatic door closers. The electrical cipher lock should also be equipped with a keyed bypass lock to allow access in the event of power failure. These lock codes should also be changed regularly.
- Key Locks - The key type padlock of brass construction with pin tumblers and a hardened shackle are generally the most satisfactory for outside use. Where possible, locks should be rekeyed, replaced, or discarded prior to a new tenant moving in.

Advanced electronic key technologies should also be considered. These systems provide a number of benefits to the user. First, electronic keys provide airport management with the ability to immediately disable access on keys that, are lost or stolen. Second, using electronic keys provide a record of users movements throughout the airport area.

Deadbolt locks, built-in door handle locks, or padlocks and metallic keys should be considered to secure an access point, particularly those that are low-risk, low throughput, or significantly distant from the main areas of concern or from the central control station. Such locking systems may involve other procedural issues, such as a key management system and the difficulties of recoring at numerous locations and the reissuing of keys when they are lost or stolen.

Of primary importance in maintaining the integrity of a locking system is the establishment of effective key control, including control of keys, key codes, key cutting and combination equipment, and key issuance and retrieval. Rigid controls should be established to ensure that:

- If systems requiring key cutting codes and equipment are used, measures are taken to protect them against loss or misuse.
- Key issuance authority is limited to as few personnel as possible to minimize improper distribution.
- Keys are issued to personnel on the basis of operational needs and not as a convenience.
- Keys are retrieved when personnel leave the airport by transfer, dismissal, resignation, or lease expiration.
- Lost keys are reported promptly to the appropriate airport personnel.
- Unissued locks and keys are properly safeguarded.
- Keys are stamped or engraved with "Do Not Duplicate".
- The key issuance system is periodically audited to ensure accountability for all keys.

An important consideration in such investments in airport equipment is total life cycle costs, not merely the initial capital cost. This is a concept that should carry over into any equipment procurement process.

Appendix D – Fencing

Security fencing is the most common means of securing a perimeter. Fencing can vary in design, height, and type depending on local security needs. Typically, fences are low-maintenance, provide clear visibility for security patrols, and are available in varieties that can be installed in almost any environment. Barbed wire, razor wire, and other available features increase intrusion difficulty. For locations with aesthetic concerns, there are also a large variety of decorative yet functional styles available, as well as opaque styles that limit public visibility of service, storage, or other non-aesthetic areas.

Fencing can vary in design and function depending on the facility. Such barriers can range from chain link fencing topped with barbed wire similar to that found at commercial service airports, to a simple split rail fence designed to alert individuals to the presence of the airport operations area. In any case, fencing will not discourage a determined intruder. However, it can serve to alert airport management to the presence of unauthorized individuals. To derive value from a fencing system, airport personnel and users must be educated in the use of a "challenge" system. A challenge system involves airport employees and users confronting unknown personnel on the airport to determine whether or not they have a valid reason for being on airport property. Such a system may include stopping and questioning or even simply greeting the unknown individual and engaging in conversation to determine their purpose for being in a restricted area.

It should be noted that while fencing is normally the most effective physical barrier for securing the airside, fencing an entire perimeter may not be economically feasible or even necessary for many airports. Partial fencing of sensitive areas such as the terminal area, aircraft storage, or maintenance areas may be more appropriate and can prove to be just as effective.

The physical security barrier provided by a fence provides the following functions[1]:

- Gives notice of the legal boundary of the outermost limits of a facility or security sensitive area.
- Assists in controlling and screening authorized entries into a secured area by deterring entry elsewhere along the boundary.
- Supports surveillance, detection, assessment, and other security functions by providing a zone for installing intrusion detection equipment and closed-circuit television (CCTV).
- Deters casual intruders from penetrating a secured area by presenting a barrier that requires an overt action to enter.

---

[1] Source: Chain Link Fence Manufacturer's Institute.

- Demonstrates the intent of an intruder by their overt action of gaining entry.
- Causes a delay to obtain access to a facility, thereby increasing the possibility of detection.
- Creates a psychological deterrent.
- Optimizes the use of security personnel while enhancing the capabilities for detection and apprehension of unauthorized individuals.
- Demonstrates a corporate concern for facility security
- Provides a cost effective method of protecting facilities

Some basic fencing features that enhance security include:

- **Height** - the higher the barrier, the more difficult and time consuming to breach.
- **Barbed Wire** - adding barbed wire at the top of the fence increases the level of difficulty and time to breach.
- **Eliminating handholds** - omitting a rail at the top of the fence makes the fence more difficult to climb.
- **Burying the bottom of the fencing** - eliminates the possibility of forcing the mesh up so that individuals can crawl under.
- **Sensor system** - addition of an intrusion/alert system adds another level of security to the perimeter.
- **Lighting** - increases visibility as well as raises the level of psychological deterrent.
- **Signage** - installed along the fence line, signs are important to indicate private secured areas and the presence of security patrols, alarms, or monitoring systems.
- **Clear areas** - security effectiveness of perimeter fencing is materially improved by the provision of clear areas on both sides of the fence, particularly in the vicinity of the terminal and any other critical facilities. Such clearance areas facilitate surveillance and maintenance of fencing and deny cover to vandals and trespassers. Suggested clear distances range from 10 to 30 feet, within which there should be no climbable objects, trees, or utility poles abutting the fence line nor areas for stackable crates, pallets, storage containers, or other materials. Likewise, the parking of vehicles along the fence should also be minimized. In addition, landscaping within the clear area should be minimized or eliminated to reduce potential hidden locations for persons, objects, fence damage, and vandalism.

There have been cases in which individuals have gained access to passenger aircraft by scaling or crashing through perimeter fencing. To deter or delay attacks, sufficient distance should be maintained between the perimeter fencing and aircraft parking areas.

However, airport operators should be careful that increased perimeter controls and measures do not prevent authorized personnel from gaining airfield access (e.g. fire and emergency response vehicles and personnel need to be assured unrestricted access).

Additional Information on materials and installation is available in FAA Advisory Circular (AC) 107-1, Aviation Security – Airports; AC 150/5360-13, Planning and Design Guidelines for Airport Terminal Facilities; AC 150/5370-10, Standards for Specifying Construction of Airports, and DOT/FAA/AR-00/52, Recommended Security Guidelines for Airport Planning, Design, and Construction.

Appendix E – Access Points

If perimeter controls are used for an airport, access points for personnel and vehicles through the boundary lines, such as gates, doors, and electronically controlled or monitored access points should also be considered. In addition, access point type and design may be the determining factor in the effectiveness of the security boundary and control in that area. So, in all cases, the number of access points should be minimized and their use and conditions regularly monitored.

Any access point through a fence or other boundary should not only be able to control or prevent access, but also differentiate between an authorized and an unauthorized user. At an airport, access through boundary lines is often quite frequent, and must be quick in order to prevent unacceptable delays. In addition, if a boundary access point is not user-friendly, it may be abused, disregarded, or subverted and thus pose a security risk. Regardless of boundary location or type, the number of access points should be minimized for both security and cost efficiency.

Gates are the only moveable part of a fence and therefore should be properly constructed with appropriate fittings. Chain link gate specifications are specified in industry and federal guidance documents listed in the bibliography. Gates should be constructed and installed to the same or greater standard of security as any adjacent fencing in order to maintain the integrity of the area. All gates should have self-closures and be equipped so that they can be secured should enhanced security conditions require it. All gates should be sufficiently lighted. Swing gate hinges should be of the non-liftoff type or provided with additional welding to prevent the gates from being removed. Security provided by gates can be improved if they are designed and installed with no more than 4-6" of ground clearance beneath the gate and minimal gaps on both sides of the gate.

For vehicle access, limiting the size of the opening increases security, reduces the possibility of one vehicle passing another and shortens the open close cycle time. The cantilever slide gate is the most effective for vehicle security especially one that is electrically operated and tied into an access control system.

"Tailgating" entry may be a concern at unstaffed vehicle access points. Tailgating involves an unauthorized vehicle closely following behind an authorized vehicle in order to pass through an access point before the gate closes. The first response to this is usually a procedural one rather than design, since it is the responsibility of the person authorized to use the gate to be certain tailgating does not occur. To reinforce the user's responsibility, the airport may elect to use signs reminding vehicle operators to confirm gate closure. However, if a fence design solution is desired, an automated two-gate system (also known as vehicle entrapment gate) is one method that can help prevent "tailgate" entry. Such gates are separated one vehicle length apart and are sequenced so that the second gate does not open until the first has fully closed. Time-delayed closures are a viable alternative. Timers can be increased or decreased to accommodate threat levels. Sensor arrays have also been used to successfully monitor vehicle movement and assist in detection of "tailgate" entries. "Tailgating" and "reverse tailgating" (where a vehicle enters a gate opened by an exiting vehicle) at automated gates may also be reduced by use of a security equipment layout that provides space for waiting vehicles to stop, which obstructs, or at least deters other vehicles from passing through.

Pedestrian/personnel gates can be constructed using a basic padlock or designed with an electrical or mechanical lock or a keypad/card key system tied into an access control system. Pre-hung pedestrian gates/portals installed independent of the fence line are available to isolate the gate from fence lines containing sensor systems, thus reducing possible false alarms.

Appendix F – Lighting

Good protective lighting is achieved by adequate, even light upon bordering areas, glaring lights oriented toward pedestrian and vehicle avenues of approach, and relatively little light on the guard personnel. Lighting units for perimeter fences should be located a sufficient distance within the protected area and above the fence so that the light pattern on the ground will include an area on both the inside and the outside of the fence. Generally, the light band should illuminate the fence perimeter barrier and extend as deeply as possible into the approach area. Limiting factors on the orientation of lights and the depth of the light band may include airport operations and air safety requirements, residences, waterways, and roadways. Types of protective lighting systems and light sources include the following:

- Continuous Lighting. This is the most common protective lighting system. It consists of a series of fixed lights arranged to flood a given area with overlapping zones of light on a continuous basis during the hours of darkness. There are two methods of employment of this system:
  - Glare projection lighting where the glare of lights directed across surrounding territory will not be annoying or interfere with adjacent operations;
  - Controlled lighting where the width of the lighted strip is restricted to meet a particular need.
- Standby Lighting. Lights in this system are either automatically or manually turned on at a prearranged time, when suspicious activity is detected, or when an interruption of power occurs.
- Movable Lighting. This type of lighting consists of manually-operated, movable flood lights.
- Emergency Lighting. This system may duplicate any of the aforementioned systems. Its use is limited to periods of power failure or other emergencies and is dependent upon an alternate power source.
- Solar Powered Lighting: In areas where electricity does not exist or is cost prohibitive solar powered lighting may be considered a viable alternative and have a wide range of applications.

Lighting of security areas on both sides of gates and selected areas of fencing is highly effective. Lighting is beneficial not only for security inspection, but also to ensure that fence/gate signage is readable and that card readers, keypads, phones, locks, and/or other devices at the gate are visible and usable. Similarly, sufficient lighting is required for any area in which a CCTV camera is intended to monitor activity. Reduced lighting or sensor activated (e.g. proximity, photoelectric, or timers) lighting may be considered in areas which have minimal traffic throughput in the off-peak hours.

Appendix G – Security Procedures Template

GA Airport Security Procedures

(Airport Name)

(Original Publication Date)

(Date Last Revised)

Table of Contents

Outline all of the sections of the document with corresponding page number for quick reference.

Section I: Disclosure Statement / Security Responsibilities

Distribution of these Security Procedures should be restricted to individuals with a legitimate need for access to them.

Identify the individual who has the responsibility for the development, upkeep and administration of the Airport Security Procedures

Section II: General Information

1. Forward

Identify the airport owner and the person(s) responsible for airport activities (e.g. State, county, authority, commission).

2. Introduction and Purpose

Provide a brief introduction that describes the purpose (what will it be used for) and the need (why was it created) for airport security procedures.

3. Distribution

You should list all individuals and agencies that will receive copies of the Airport Security Procedures.

Example:
- State / Local Police Department
- Fixed Base Operator
- Individual Tenants

4. Name and Location of Airport

- Airport Name
- Airport Address
- Normal Business / 24-hour Emergency / Fax Phone Number
- Airport Identifier
- Proximity to nearest major city. List the city and provide a state location map as an attachment.
- Airport Geographical Coordinates: latitude, longitude, elevation.

5. Airport Activities

- Types of flight activities (e.g. flight school, State Police, corporate)
- Hours of operation
- Number of annual operations
- Number of based aircraft

6. Airport Description

- Size: List the size of the airport in approximate acres or square miles.
- Runways, Taxiways, Ramps: Identify runways and their dimensions, taxiways, and ramp areas: Provide an airport layout plan / diagram as an attachment.
- Buildings:
    o List the number and types of buildings (offices, hangars, maintenance shops).
    o List the primary tenants for each of the buildings.
- Airport Tenants:
    o List hours of operation
    o List primary and emergency contact information
- Other Airport Facilities

7. Emergency Phone Numbers:

List all appropriate emergency contact numbers. Include point of contact names and office hours of operation as appropriate (e.g. FSD, alternate contacts).

- All Emergencies   911
- State Police (non-emergency)
- Local Police (non-emergency)
- Local Fire Department
- Airport Director (24 hour contact)
- Airport Facility Supervisor (pager)
- State / Local Aviation Official
- Federal Bureau of Investigation Local Field Office
- FAA Flight Standards District Office (FSDO)
- TSA Airport Watch Hot-Line   866-427-3287
- Local TSA Federal Security Director

Section III: Definitions and Terms

It may be useful to include a list of frequently used terminology to enhance clarity within the document.

Section IV: Administration

1. Airport Operator: List who operates the airport.

2. Individual responsible for airport security

   List the responsibilities of this individual. These duties may include:

   - Timely provision of evidence of security measure compliance as may be requested.
   - Maintaining a complete and current list of all individuals with airport access.
   - Maintaining documentation of all training provided in accordance with any current Airport Security Procedures.
   - Maintaining and updating the Airport Security Procedures to reflect the current state of conditions at the airport.
   - Timely distribution of the Airport Security Procedures or specific parts thereof, to appropriate persons or entities.
   - Proper dissemination of all correspondence or other communications with airport tenants and others on security related matters.
   - Daily oversight of security provisions at the airport and ensuring compliance with the Security Procedures.

Section V: Aircraft Movement Area / Security Control

1. Aircraft Movement Area
   Describe any area that may be used for landing, take-off, and surface maneuvering of aircraft including all intermediate unpaved sections of the airfield encompassed on the airport property. You should also include a map or diagram as an attachment.

2. Describe any perimeter barriers or access controls such as:
   - Fencing
   - Gates
   - Access Control System
   - Airport Locks
   - Key Control System

Section VI: Airport Security Procedures

Describe any Airport Security Procedures such as:
- Aircraft security requirements
- Pedestrian/vehicle access
- Challenge procedures
- Reporting of suspicious behavior

Section VII: Airport Emergency Grid Map

Airport operators may also wish to consider creating an emergency locator map. The map should identify all relevant areas of the airport on a grid map such as:

- Runways
- Ramp areas
- Fence line
- Gates
- Automobile parking areas
- Hydrants
- Emergency shelters
- Buildings
- Hazardous materials sites

This map should be provided to emergency response personnel (fire, EMS, etc.) and law enforcement as well as airport personnel.

Section VIII: Identification of Airport Personnel

Describe any personnel identification methods/systems and the procedures for those that are currently in use. Such as:

- Airport-issued identification badge(s) or card(s)
- Identification Badge / Card application procedures
- Other acceptable forms of identification
- Accountability of lost/stolen identification badges / cards
- Temporary airport identification badges / cards
- Uniforms which display logo or other identifiable markings

Section IX: Identification of Vehicles

Describe what methods/systems are used to identify authorized vehicles in the air operations area. The following are examples of methods to identify authorized vehicles:

- Special paint schemes or markings
- Decal in a specified location on the vehicle
- Hang tags

Section X: Law Enforcement

Describe any agreement(s) and responsibilities that the airport owner/operator(s) may have with law enforcement agencies to provide support, traffic control, police patrols and any emergency responses. Include any written agreements as attachments to the Airport Security Procedures.

Also include any methods or systems used (e.g. radios, communications channels, etc.) to directly communicate with law enforcement personnel.

Section XI: Special Events

Describe any procedures that exist for special events such as:

- Air shows
- VIP Visits
- Events that result in unusual numbers of people on the airport.

Section XII: Increased Security Threats

Describe how security measures are implemented in accordance with the raising and lowering of the Homeland Security Advisory System as described in this Information Publication in Section 3.5.2.

Section XIII: Aviation Security Contingency Plans

Identify and describe all contingency plans and procedures established for security incidents such as:

- Bomb Threats (Bomb Threat Checklist is provided as an example)
- Civil Disturbances & Crowd Control
- Air Piracy (Hijacking) Actual or Attempted
- Suspicious/Unidentified Items

Bomb Threat Call Checklist

Fill out completely, immediately after bomb threat

Exact wording of the threat:

Questions to ask:
When is the bomb going to explode?
What kind of bomb is it?
What will cause it to explode?
Did you place the bomb?
Why?
What is your address?
What is your name?

Sex of caller		Age		Race		Length of call	

Caller's voice (circle all that apply):						
Calm	Laughing	Lisp	Disguised	Angry	Crying	Raspy
Accent	Excited	Normal	Deep	Slow	Distinct	Ragged
Slurred	Nasal	Soft	Loud	Stutter	Clearing Throat	
Deep Breathing		Cracking Voice		Other:		

If voice was familiar, whom did it sound like?	

Background Sounds (Circle all that apply):				
Street Noises	House Noises	Factory	Motor	Machinery
Long Distance	Voice	Office	Animal Noises	Clear
Music	Static	P.A. System	Other:	

Threat Language (circle all that apply):				
Well Spoken	Foul	Incoherent	Educated	Irrational
Message delivered by:	Recording	Threat maker		

Remarks:

REPORT CALL IMMEDIATELY TO 911

Person who received the call	Phone
Position	

Appendix H - Bibliography

This document provides numerous references and citations to other government and industry sources. These are not intended to be modified by this document in any way, and are generally intended to refer to the most current version of such external resources, to which the reader should go for detailed information.

FAA Advisory Circulars

The latest issuance of the following advisory circulars may be obtained from the Department of Transportation, Utilization and Storage Section, M-443.2, Washington, D.C. 20590: [Also see the FAA internet web site at www.faa.gov]

1. 00-2, Advisory Circular Checklist - Contains a listing of all current advisory circulars.
2. 107-1, Aviation Security-Airports - Provides guidance and recommendations for establishing and improving airport security.*
3. 108-1, Air Carrier Security. Provides information and guidance on the implementation of Airplane Operator Security.*
4. 109-1, Aviation Security Acceptance and Handling Procedures-Indirect Air Carrier Security. Provides guidance and information for use by indirect aircraft operators when accepting and handling property to be carried by aircraft operators or by the operator of any civil aircraft for transportation in air commerce.*
5. 129-3, Foreign Air Carrier Security. Provides information and guidance on the implementation foreign air carrier security.*
6. 150/5200-31A, Airport Emergency Plan
7. 150/5300-13, Airport Design
8. 150/5360-13, Planning and Design Guidelines for Airport Terminal Facilities. Furnishes guidance material for the planning and design of airport terminal buildings and related facilities.
9. 150/5370-10, Standards for Specifying Construction of Airports

* - On November 19, 2001, Congress enacted the Aviation and Transportation Security Act (ATSA), Public Law 107–71, 115 Stat. 597, which established the TSA. Pursuant to ATSA, the TSA became responsible for security in all modes of transportation, including civil aviation under Chapter 449 of title 49, United States Code, related research and development activities, and other transportation security functions exercised by DOT. Consequently 14 CFR parts 107, 108, 109, and certain provisions of part 129 were removed and transferred into the relevant parts of 49 CFR 1542, 1544, 1548, and 1546 respectively. While the materials referenced here are related to superceded regulations, they may still provide relevant information and have therefore been included.

U.S. Government Regulations

The TSA issues and administers Transportation Security Regulations (TSRs), which are codified in Title 49 of the Code of Federal Regulations (CFR), Chapter XII, parts 1500 through 1699. Many TSRs are former rules of the Federal Aviation Administration (FAA) that were transferred to TSA when TSA assumed FAA's civil aviation security function on February 17, 2002. [All of these regulations can be found at http://www.tsa.gov/].

It should be clearly noted that these regulations pertain mainly to regulated entities and not typically to GA operators or facilities and are provided for reference and informational purposes only.

1. **49 CFR Part 1540** Civil Aviation Security: General Rules - This part contains rules that cover all segments of civil aviation security. It contains definitions that apply to Subchapter C, and it contains rules that apply to passengers, aviation employees, and other individuals and persons related to civil aviation security, including airport operators, aircraft operators, and foreign air carriers.
2. **49 CFR Part 1542** Airport Security - This Part requires airport operators to adopt and carry out a security program approved by TSA. It describes requirements for security programs, including establishing secured areas, air operations areas, security identification display areas, and access control systems. This Part also contains requirements for fingerprint based criminal history record checks of specified individuals. This part describes the requirements related to Security Directives issued to airport operators.
3. **49 CFR Part 1544** Aircraft Operator Security: Air Carriers and Commercial Operators - This Part applies to certain aircraft operators holding operating certificates for scheduled passenger operations, public charter passenger operations, private charter passenger operations, and other aircraft operators. This Part requires such operators to adopt and carry out a security program approved by TSA. It contains requirements for screening of passengers and property. This Part also describes requirements applicable to law enforcement officers flying armed aboard an aircraft, as well as requirements for fingerprint based criminal history record checks of specified individuals. This Part describes the requirements related to Security Directives issued to aircraft operators.
4. **49 CFR Part 1550** Aircraft Security Under General Operating and Flight Rules - This part applies to the operation of aircraft for which there are no security requirements in other Parts of Chapter XII, including general aviation aircraft.

Other Reports

1. Recommended Security Guidelines for Airport Planning, Design and Construction, DOT/FAA/AR-00/52, Federal Aviation Administration, June 2001.

2. Report of the GA Airports Security Working Group, Aviation Security Advisory Committee, October 1, 2003.
3. GA Airport Security Task Force Recommendations, American Association of Airport Executives, June 2002.
4. GA Security, National Association of State Aviation Officials, December 2002.

Appendix I – Useful Websites

Aviation Trade Associations

Organization	Website
Aircraft Owners and Pilots Association	www.aopa.org
Airports Consultants Council	www.acconline.org
American Association of Airport Executives	www.aaae.com
Experimental Aircraft Association	www.eaa.org
GA Manufacturers Association	www.gama.aero
Helicopter Association International	www.rotor.com
National Agricultural Aircraft Association	www.agaviation.org
National Air Transportation Association	www.nata-online.org
National Association of State Aviation Officials	www.nasao.org
National Business Aviation Association	www.nbaa.org
United States Parachute Association	www.uspa.org

Federal Government

Organization	Website
Department of Homeland Security	www.dhs.gov
Federal Aviation Administration	www.faa.gov
Federal Bureau of Investigation	www.fbi.gov
Transportation Security Administration	www.tsa.gov

Other References

Organization	Website
ASIS International (Industrial security organization)	www.asisonline.org
Aviation Crime Prevention Institute	www.acpi.org
Chain Link Fence Manufacturers Institute	http://codewriters.com/asites/main-pub.cfm?usr=clfma